Simmer Dim

Akron Series in Poetry

Akron Series in Poetry

Elton Glaser, Editor

Barry Seiler, *The Waters of Forgetting*

Raeburn Miller, *The Comma After Love:
Selected Poems of Raeburn Miller*

William Greenway, *How the Dead Bury the Dead*

Jon Davis, *Scrimmage of Appetite*

Anita Feng, *Internal Strategies*

Susan Yuzna, *Her Slender Dress*

Raeburn Miller, *The Collected Poems of Raeburn Miller*

Clare Rossini, *Winter Morning with Crow*

Barry Seiler, *Black Leaf*

William Greenway, *Simmer Dim*

Jeanne E. Clark, *Ohio Blue Tips*

Simmer
Dim

WILLIAM GREENWAY

The University of Akron Press
Akron, Ohio

For Betty, and for all of our friends in Wales

Acknowledgments: *Envoi:* "Mumbles," "Simmer Dim," "Llyn y Fan Fach," "Scissors on Sunday"; *Ekphrasis:* "In the Musée d'Orsay"; *Fine Madness:* "Remains to Be Seen" (as "Cornwall"); *Haiku Quarterly:* "The Fish Shop That Faced the Sun"; *The Literary Review:* "Simmer Dim"; *Many Mountains Moving:* "Creature"; *Missouri Review:* "Now That It's Over," "The Train to Neath," "Footpaths," "At Arthur's Stone," "Teeth Will Be Provided"; *New Welsh Review:* "Fancy View," "Forecast," "Blodeuwedd," "At Arthur's Stone," "Self-burial," "Cavan Girl," "Hooks"; *New Zoo Poetry Review:* "Creature"; *Nimrod:* "Blodeuwedd," "Pwll Du," "Scissors on Sunday," "Welsh Courier Braves Daylight"; *Parting Gifts:* "Depth of Field"; *Poem:* "Bread of Heaven," "Forecast"; *Poetry:* "Progress"; *Poetry Wales:* "Worm's Head"; *Rain in Most Places*, March Street Press (chapbook): "Forecast," "Remains to be Seen" (as "Cornwall"), "Under Sir John's Hill," and "There"; *Shenandoah:* "The Vines"; *Slant:* "Inverness"; *Southern Review:* "The Silkie," "In the Old Neighborhood"; *Yarrow:* "The Children of Rhys the Deep."

"Now That It's Over," "The Train to Neath," "Footpaths," "At Arthur's Stone," and "Teeth Will Be Provided" won the 1997 Editors' Prize from *Missouri Review*.

With many thanks to all of our friends in the Dylan Thomas Society of Great Britain.

I thank Youngstown State University for the sabbatical year that allowed me to write this book.

All inquiries and permissions requests should be addressed to the Publisher, The University of Akron Press, 374B Bierce Library, Akron, Ohio 44325-1703.

Library of Congress Cataloging-in-Publication Data
Greenway, William, 1947
    Simmer dim / William Greenway. — 1st ed.
    p. cm. — (Akron series in poetry)
    ISBN 1-884836-41-0 (cloth : alk. paper)
    ISBN 1-884836-42-9 (pbk. : alk. paper)
    I. Title. II. Series.
    PS3557.R3969 S5 1999
    811'.54—ddc21   98-45412
                    CIP

Manufactured in the United States of America

First Edition

Contents

V. The Last Holiday

ONE

The Once and Future Wales

Footpaths

Jon Anderson, my Jo Jon
We've climbed the hill together,
And many a canty day, Jon,
We've had with one another.

—Robert Burns

This is why we came, these tracks
through farmyard and field, around
rusted harrows as the farmers work,
their border collies crazy-eyed at us
as two more things to organize, direct,
although our feet already trace
the steps of sheep and cows, between
the green pools of slurry, here
where fence nor nothing private
can stop us legally, because the dead,
lying in the churchyards of these valleys,
have stamped a seal into this clay
and put a stile over every obstacle.

Even in dreams, I follow
a stenciled yellow arrow on the walls
of train stations, into toilets, over stiles,
through a window into an alley,
nowhere I can't go, until the trees
thicken and I can't fit between or through
contractions of a farmhouse window,
my body inside, my head left stuck
on the sill, cooling like a pie.

We've walked hundreds of miles like this;
our maps, weary at the fold,
we point like dueling compasses,

our shadows hesitating
on the sundial of a field,
our feet always after another
dotted line or hedged-in lane.
We know how long a wrong turn takes,
have come to hate the forks,
and tire of saying *the road not taken.*

We travel well, you say;
it's home where we get lost.
On the tops of hills, our breathing slow,
we've learned the price of every view,
and measure our desire against
the steeper climb, the even steeper fall,
where the knees almost want to fail,
give in, to just let go and run,
as if we'd be able to stop.

The colors this November
still have a way to go,
and though the summer was warmer
than ever before, the winter
has taken no offense so far.
Has a winter ever never happened?
They say there's a valley near
no frost has ever touched,
and though we have no map,
why should that stop us now?
As long as we can see at least the ghosts
of other steps across the field,
let's take this path through woods,
and the long climb over the hill.

Welsh Courier Braves Daylight

for John

The book we ordered didn't come in.
It didn't get put
on the van, she says.
Maybe next week.

Things are different here.
We order our turkey
from Rhys the Meat
who hands it to us
in a flurry of feathers,
though he doesn't know why,
or what Thanksgiving is.
The little watchmaker,
in his element
of Dickensian ticking,
declines to tackle
my electric watch.
The fishmonger says,
I don't know.
Crabs is crabs.
The kind with little legs.

Out on the blue bay
draining to low tide,
fishing boats bob
to find bottom;
wild ponies have picked the gate
to eat our garden,
and sheep wander the roads
like blown batting.
Our e-mail won't work,

and for fax and photocopy
we go down to the village,
to the model train store.
I watch the tiny cars trace rails
through matchbox coal towns
and pipe-cleaner trees.

We're living here this year
five time zones away
from all we thought,
and if we miss something
we've learned to let it go,
to have another pint,
knowing whatever it is
just might come on the van
next week, or around the cape
if the seas are mild,
or on muleback
if the snows don't clog the pass.

Llyn y Fan Fach

for Nigel

It means in Welsh the small lake of the high
ground, or something, all their places
hallowed with words of what or where or why—

*St. Mary's Church in a hollow by the white
hazel close to the rapid whirlpool,*
etc., or stories of what might

have been. Here, a woman with a golden comb
rose from a lake in a lap of mountains
to let a poor and lonely farmer take her home,

only to return, when she had paid her debt
of love, taking her sheep and oxen back
to the waters closed forever on a story of regret.

All of it meaning something else down deep,
like the forest underneath our feet that day
already up to the chapter on peat

and climbing on to the coal and steep
diamond denouement. We'd hiked
the gravel path through red-daubed sheep

halfway up Wales to the highest view,
and though we've always told ourselves
You never regret the things you do,

only the things you don't, that bare hill
glowered down at us until we took
our boots off, stuck our feet into the chill

fairy woman's world, though not stripping
to swim, to join our Welsh friend blowing
and splashing, a young and dripping

Welsh Whitman, and we declined to climb to where
the brow of mountain beetled over all
of lonely Wales that clear, rare,

cloudless day, and back we walked without the end
of the story, talking of the folktales of America
instead, telling our impulsive friend

how Paul Bunyan made the Mississippi with his ax
and ox, of Johnny Appleseed, the pioneers,
the tiny graves beside the rutted tracks

of wagon trains, the tragedies of travel,
and hearing through ourselves, in the interval of words,
the mewling of sheep and the gnawing of gravel.

Fancy View

We have lunch in the crater
of a green moonscape,
guessing what—glacier, bomb,
the forestry service?—has made it
then soothed it over
like a nightmare putting green
and planted around the lip
of this cup holding our picnic table
a golden picket of young birches,
a fort I would have loved as a boy
with long October afternoons to spend.

Up a steep climb is the "Fancy View,"
through blue haze the rust of autumn
on hills like the Georgia Smokies
where my grandfather settled because,
red dirt and all, they reminded him
of the hills of Wales he saw as a boy
coming up, at the end of the day,
in a cage from the mine.

On the walk down is a plaque
drilled into golden stone
showing beneath us the squirm
of mines, the hills around us slag tips,
telling how boys woke at four
and walked five miles in the dark
to pull all day on their knees
through tunnels the sleds of coal,
and, going home, played rugby
by the pit-light of the moon,
how hostlers fed the horses

in the cold down there,
only bringing them up for strikes,
then taking them back down for good.

Our faces lie on the glass
of a few old, smoky photographs
of machines, mustached men
in bowler hats and suits,
and black-faced boys too small
for the miners' lamps they wear,
and we walk more carefully, lightly,
back to the car as if our weight
might crush the tunnels riddling
underneath our feet,
keeping everything down forever.

Pwll Du

for Wally

Through caves of oak and beech, I walk a mile
above the stream that sinks and wanders
underground through limestone for a while

before it surges from the hill
into the clear, blue air of beach
and merges with the sea, now still.

The path, too, bursts into sun and rain
from out of moldy leaves and gloom of wood,
to cliffs where you can breathe again.

And there below is the quiet bay
where the weekend cottages once were pubs
when the quarry worked in golden days

and money brought men here. Now dogs
chase the creamy surf for sticks,
while lovers lie by driftwood logs,

and the old continually watch the tide
to see what washes up, as if
for consolation from the other side.

Above the beach, below the hill, alone,
is a grave of men, their only monument
a ragged ring of quarry stone

laid beneath the bracken of this cape.
The others never found, just sixty-eight
lie within a giant footstep shape

because one afternoon, against their will,
they disappeared from Swansea streets
to live an hour at sea until

the ship in sea wrack struck the rocks.
The crew survived, but left them there below
in chains, their feet in stocks.

The transcript of the trial effaced the dead,
no mention made of men impressed;
the ship alone was lost, the record said.

Sometimes there is no metaphor,
analogy, or rhyme,
and reason winks its semaphore

at fog "shrouding" the mast,
waves "clawing" at the ship.
No elegy could hope to last

as long as lines of stones,
the want of name on every one
as elegant, articulate as bones.

And yet I say, *As bones*, as if I doubt
the things I see and feel
and cannot find them real without

another name, as ships are called
Endeavor, Self Reliant, Hope,
as if the words forestalled

the salted eyes and stolen breath,
the water at our feet, our waist,
rising like the certainty of death.

Never proper sailors like the rest
who lived or died at sea,
their signatures upon a manifest,

these men were on no list of any kind—
picked at random, stones were gathered,
aligned, and left behind.

I etch on each the names, like metaphor:
Water Filling His Mouth,
Forgotten, and *Forevermore.*

The Fish Shop That Faced the Sun

for Eryl

But then, his fish shop faced the sun,
you see, she says, speaking of someone
long gone, someone I never knew,
though I see on shaved ice
the fire hoses of conger eels,
white rubbery rays,
pink commas of prawns,
chevrons of trout sheening
in poor shade, mouths sulking, eyes
cataracting.

Here, you are your work—
Dai the Bread, Morgan the Milk,
Fred the Death.
Through the window of Dylan's pub,
men on the dole watch the sands
of Swansea Bay, where cocklers have
only once a day to dig.
Down the road the curry house is closed,
mail piling up beneath the slot,
behind the glass door. *Taxes,*
someone says, like the record of failure
everywhere—the tide coming in,
erasing the scribbles of the cockle men,
wind and waves in the fisherman's face,
air to the fish, too much rain
to the wheat, spring onions in the milk.
She says he had no luck, his wife running away
to London. And, of course, the sun in the afternoon.
The stink beginning, you see. The waste
of things thrown out too soon.

The Train to Neath

Like lantern blur through fog, we ride
across the coal-dust river to
the cinder bank of the other side,

almost disembodied, dead,
gliding along aloof and looking
over garden walls and into potting sheds,

past flowered council housing shades
to rooms where peat fires smoke and photos
on the mantels craze and fade.

The backs hold sticks of broken winter frames
whose shards of hothouse glass infect
a knacker's yard of furniture gone lame

after the mines were closed. Now coal
is scarce, the union hall is used
for bingo, everyone is on the dole.

We watch as lovers mime goodbyes into the dark;
the conductor stamps our tickets with his cross,
or ankh—he thinks we want to disembark,

instead of this continued opportunity
of sliding past and looking at
eye-level life with insular impunity,

like the cushioned joints we barely feel,
the rails so close but still detached,
thumping out their muffled pairs of wheels

like heartbeats under wool, a demi-death—
the double panes of windows holding back
our words but showing us our breath.

The Meeting

The baby's pointed ears and pixie hair
are throwbacks, like her black
eyes and sideways smile, a pair
of genes traveling here from way back

then, like salmon up the years.
And so we hail the conference theme and toast
the Once and Future Wales with endless beers
at this meeting on the Celtic coast.

Silurian and crafty, always hiding
as of old, she's quiet, small, and fey,
as when the taller, fairer Celts came riding
roughshod in to steal the land away,

never really seen, but sighted, only found
at edges, at the boundaries,
tylwyth teg, the little people living underground;
the tall ones called them fairies.

Because they didn't know
how to make the age's iron, they hid
in "hollow hills" and never learned, and so
they died beneath the swords of those who did.

They crept into the house at night and stole,
because they had none of their own, it's said,
a human baby for its soul
and left a changeling in the cot instead.

Taffy is a liar,
Taffy is a thief.

The only child I've ever wanted,
she sleeps and smiles the endless meetings through,
a little black-haired person—haunted,
perhaps, by perfect memories—who

never cries, but listens, looks
not at you, but beyond your face
at somewhere only read about in books,
at something in some other place.

Come away, O human child!
To the waters and the wild.

All the weekend as we've met, I've sat
and mostly dozed and dreamed as all
discussed the Welsh of this and that.
Though I am dark and tall,

the tall genes stop with me for good,
as do the darker Welsh ones too,
and thus my chance at Celtic fatherhood.
I'm just the sort of Taffy who,

like *tylwyth teg*, reclusive, sly,
dreams about the woods and wild,
who loves to tell a lie,
to Welsh, to steal a child.

TWO

Bread of Heaven

At Arthur's Stone

for Gilbert

They say on simmer dim this stone will stand
then walk the long slope down to Burry to drink.
At the winter solstice, hand-in-hand

for now, the truce between us holding for a while,
we walk the frosted rusty red
of autumn fern, past a moldering pile

of wild Welsh pony bones
to see the grave of an early king,
a stone balanced long ago on other stones.

We touch its blotched, gray flank
as millions have, for luck,
as though solidity and poise, its blank

face could cure us of our yearnings, keep
our lives together till we die.
Nearby's a cairn of those like us, a heap

of stones too numerous to name, too small
to walk, that marks the grave of men
who dragged or sailed it here to rest on tall

and humpbacked Cefn Bryn, to overlook the bay
of cockle sands that glisten when the tide is out,
and be the shrine of girls who came to lay

milk-soaked honey cake upon the ground
before this altar stone,
and crawl three times around—

if her love were true, he would appear,
transported from whatever distant place,
easing through the mist to meet her here.

The moon comes up behind a pony white
as a unicorn, the sun goes down
and pinks the sky and bay before the night

recalls this postcard from the past.
Too far away to see the cars
and houses with their shipwreck masts

of washing poles and satellite dishes,
we might be a pelted pair of ancient,
shivering, short-lived, walking wishes

staring at the mound where we will lie.
And every longest day, the sun
will squint between the lids of sea and sky

that never close, and from this height—
as we dream our centuries of thirst
through the long, dying light—

like a mote in an eye that cannot blink,
the stone of one who lost his love
will walk to the sea to drink.

Teeth Will Be Provided

The breath of all those sermons
blows down these valleys like the fog,
like a hymn when the wind makes organ
music of the ruined houses, bouldered hills.
As the son and grandson of one
of the Welsh who would *hwyl* hellfire,
I recognize the chapel gloom that hangs
and falls like night in the winter by four.

My grandfather passed down *no*'s
to my father who put them in me
where I carry them into middle age,
no way around the coal-dust darkness
of a Sabbath parlor or the leather strop
of Bible cover, taking even to Georgia's
new Eden fire and brimstone to light
satanic cotton mills, fluorescent
sanctuaries of Southern Baptist Sunday night.

*There's the world's way
and the Lord's way,* they used to say—
from pulpit or the car's front seat—
of scout camp, liquor, cards,
Ed Sullivan on Sunday,
or the dancing of the senior prom
where bellies rubbed to saxophones,
and later in the car's front seat on country roads,
the honeysuckle scent of guilt.

No way around it, like the joke
from back when thousands pressed to hear
an evangelist chanting of hell

and the Bible's *wailing and gnashing of teeth,*
till one old-timer, like a teenage smartass, called,
But what if some of us have no teeth?
The laughter, then, and the quiet.
And then the preacher's thundering answer,
as always.

Power in the Blood

Cleaning out my father's office,
I kept humming his favorite hymn,
"Throw Out the Lifeline."
Maybe I saw it in a yellowed
sermon he never got to preach.
At his funeral, I lasted till the second verse—
When we've been there ten thousand years,
bright shining as the sun.

Here on the coast of Wales,
where it started with my grandfather
in chapels up the smoky valleys,
on cliffs I've learned the need
of clefts in rock, anything to block
the wind, I've seen the lifeboat
flume to the waves and heard, from a room
of whiskey and candlelight,
the boom of the lifeline rocket
flaring in the storm.

Are you washed in the blood? we'd ask
each other every Sunday night,
sing *throw out the lifeline*
while the rest of the heathen world
watched *The Wizard of Oz,*
or the Beatles on Ed Sullivan,
or sat in a bar, or wrote their poems.
Monday morning found my mother
back on her knees, scrubbing, scrubbing,
slapping me for muddy shoes, insolent
prints on the polished mahogany.

Even now, I'm contemptuous
of those who try to make their own religion,
hate Sunday nights, the lonely, straying
ones who end alone and childless
in furnished, rented rooms, writing
letters to the editor, or poems,
peculiar, faithless souls who sing
late into the night the drunken hymns
of childhood, where tomorrow's sun
may never shine, and clothes, when washed
in blood, grow white as snow.

Elegy from a Drunk Tank

Driving home last night, way
past closing time, past all
the bleary headlights
of the two-lane county road,
I thought of him a half a world—
and six feet down—away,
still blond and tall and strong,
I bet, Apollo, like a negative
of me, my cousin nine years dead.

Born the same year (our mothers
sibling rivals), I was the first
to walk the aisle "Just As I Am,"
the preacher's son, he the jock,
the first to fuck a girl.
But he became the man of God
who went unto the world to spread
the word, while I just spread with beer
and turned my face from the true light.

Weaving home last night, maudlin,
I sobbed until the headlights smeared,
thinking of the nights we lay
side by side as on a tomb.
Why cry if he's in heaven?
Why whine, or wine, when I've had
nine more years than he whose life
was plucked from a country road,
clean as the twang of a snapped guitar string,
who, like the Bible Paul, was caught head-on,
though not in holy spotlight,
but in the bloodshot headlight

of a drunken shotgunned pickup,
while *my* god, grape-leaved, gentle,
here in Wales, always waits
by the road for me,
his blue light softly flashing.
I pull in slow and raise my hands.

The Bodies of Poets

If only I could floss my liver
tonight, or tomorrow whip
my heart to a peg-leg beat along
a one-lane country road, that strip

of lonely grass in the middle, and set
my eyes to the shape of trees at twilight.
If only there were rain enough
to blur things right,

a streetlight-steady yellow moon,
or wind to hollow my head to an empty shell
for a foghorn full of the ocean's greatest hits,
what we couldn't do, we two, or stories tell,

if only I could wake all night to write
and then not lumber around all day
but up-buck, back-bounce, limber
over all the stony ways

of words, each cobble like
a little skull of doubt
in roads that squirm and bend
to just more tangled lines about

getting lost or heading for a certain end.
If only I could swallow sleeping like a seed,
grow dreams that someday warm someone,
like sheep nibbling bare a hill, succeed

at twisting tongue around a truth
to make it lasting as a lie,

continue in some speaking form,
so when I lay me down to die

before I wake, I pray the world
forget my soul, but take
and eat this meat, this beat-up
sacrament, broken for my sake.

Self-burial

These feeble pilgrims trekked so far
to reach this chapel just to die,
dragging threadbare deaths across
the hills of half of Wales to lie,

the three of them together, in the gloom
of yews to make a row of moldy tombs.
Now the congregation's gone away,
leaving crumbled, roofless rooms.

The glazier and ropemaker sat and watched
the mason carve their narrow stones—
a cross of rope on top, the lattice look
of leaded glass, and then his own,

with lines like ribs, crossed hands, some rings.
And when they died, he closed their eyes and laid
them down and covered them, then somehow pulled
on top of him the ton of slab he'd made,

a perfect fit, no fingers caught outside
to line like chicken bones a fox's den,
with nothing left beyond the graves
to body forth the deaths of private men.

I wonder how a man today
could die alone with friends, with grace,
with nothing crucial left behind,
no mess about the dying place,

just stones, and vines so tangled, old,
they're gnarled as Michelangelo's,

those naked humans, twined and holding on
to one another as the oceans rose.

Over stiles and past the arks of barns,
the bishop visits once a year,
walking through the muddy fields to hold
a wafer out to pilgrims coming here,

like us, who'll bury friends, and old,
alone, our journey done, will go half-starved
to lie beneath the weight of stone,
the one we, all our lives, have carved.

Scissors on Sunday

for Glenys

We sit around the table of food
and wine beneath the walls of what
she's cut and painted, wondering why
she has to make her different shapes
of paper, if it comes from all
those long, Welsh chapel Sundays,
a girl creeping the silent yard,
around the house of grown-ups dozing,
puffed with roast and spuds,
sprung from collars and stays.
She was forbidden a ball, a doll,
no scissors on the Sabbath, even
the swings of the village playground chained,
never mind the preacher's *Suffer the little children,*
the poor man's ox in the ditch.

Not knives carving flesh from bone,
not spoons knocking in the bowls,
but scissors—a slicing
through the pattern's onion skin,
cutting the cloth to its human shape,
one blade against another,
sharpening as it separates part from part,
the small piece from the whole.

Bread of Heaven

As I walked out under this first spring day,
tower bells tolled an old hymn,
in my memory a heaven of Welsh miners,
their mouths open like baby birds.
They remind me how far I've come
from chapel, how what I worship now
is more the mouths themselves,
so hungry for something from a great
mute God throned elsewhere.
It's hunger now that's sweet for me,
voices surpassing what they sing to
or for, the only god our great
emptiness the wind makes music of.
Mozart and Shakespeare are, finally,
their pain, out of chapel, swaying
all night on the moor, on the frozen thorn.
The birds build nests again this year
for babies that are born to freeze or fly,
either way their hearts agape,
while I worship not a God of light
but yearning itself, that has many
sweet voices, sweetest as they die,
and pray to the dark god that made
the world and lets it cry.

THREE

The Vines

Now That It's Over

They called him Lucky Leg
after he bought a butcher shop
with the war wound check,
but in the picture he's just David Wilson
planted on both feet,
a salmon holding his hands apart
like yarn. Isn't he proud, though,
as if he knew we'd be looking back
to when they grew that big?
Like that ghost out at Rhossili,
in the old stone house on the cliff by the sea,
who speaks sometimes on winter nights
when the gales are blowing,
as you read by the fire, suddenly
the cold at your back becoming breath
warm in your ear, whispering,
Why won't you turn and look at me?

Blodeuwedd

There's a folktale here of a lonely man
who married a woman, wizard-woven,
her name Blodeuedd, Welsh for flowers.
He held her in his arms like a long
bouquet, like the leggy roses
of beauty queens.

Like the one I cut my wrists for,
who danced with another boy.
Like the one here in this other land
thirty years along,
though I'm too tired and old
to bleed again.

You know what comes next—
roses prone to withering,
to falling petal by petal
from their stems—
she was fragile and fell
in love with someone else.

So his wizard father, angry,
tweaked her name a letter more
and from flowers she was made
a flowerface, the owl,
doomed to fly with chrysanthemum eyes
alone at night and shunned
by other birds.

End of story. As Arthur lost
to Lancelot, with good grace, Guinevere,
who ended alone in a nunnery,

the hills and woods outside her cell
blurred with fog like a bridal veil.

Now he must lie by the side
of a new, white bride, and hear
the small rain whisper on the windowpanes,
listen through the bare-leaved
twined-with-ivy trunks
and branches of the winter woods
for the sound a punished woman makes,
her wings flailing at the dark air
like twining fingers in her lover's hair,
crying, not who, who, who,
but still, even now, where, where?

Springsteen in Gubbio

Tonight, at home in Youngstown,
they're watching the Boss, in town
to sing his hit, "Youngstown."
And the Indians and the Braves
made it to the Series. What odds?

Here in Wales, we sit by the fire
and imagine him singing of the steel mills
amid the glow of steel mill stacks,
remembering the time I talked
you out of buying tickets
because I didn't want to stay
up all night, maybe drive in snow.
Counterfeit, I said, and you laid down
the keys and closed the door,
sat down, and graded more papers.

Four years later, we saw him
tour for *Lucky Town*,
but it wasn't the same.
We never saw Gubbio, either—
no narrow, winding, Umbrian roads
at night for *me*, I said.

Oh love, there is a special place
in heaven, in hell.
I'll go there gladly,
Barry Manilow every Vegas night,
sit broke and bloodshot in the glare
that never dies,
while you dance far above me,
Springsteen rocking all night
among the glowing towers of Gubbio.

Worm's Head

He who loves, gives a hostage to fortune.
—Nietzsche

Halfway up Rhossili Down,
the fight turns serious,
and I, as usual, go back,
leave you to climb the rest
of the bare flank alone.
I sit in our room with a view,
and because I've never wanted you more,
here, on the double bed, I try to spot you
up on the bouldered moonscape,
somewhere high above the sea,
though my eyes, bat-blind
at the best of times, can't make you out.

Waiting, I walk the flat path
out to the head the Vikings
called the *wurm*, dragon, like the carved
prows of their ships sailing away.
Looking back over my shoulder
to watch the body you're walking over,
the bracken bloody in November evening light,
I pray the thin membrane
we've known about for years won't finally give,
with me not there to hold you,
to brush the hair from your white, sleeping face.

Walking back, everything reminds me
of my fear—my shadow shooting ahead
and over the cliff, the single seagull
on symbolic ledge, the boy

fishing the dark, rising tide
from the crumbling rocks below,
wind scuffing the sea as if to mend
a puncture. The ram that's broken through
the smallest tear in the hedge, and though
alone with all that long, lovely grass,
runs desperately and aimlessly
in the space that is suddenly everywhere.

Mumbles

You surely knew that instead
of harrumphs of land edging out to sea,
the original word meant breasts, Latin, *mammae.*
The long arm of shore curving out along
the bay to these two white humps,
the lacy erection of Victorian pier,
and the lighthouse like a stout bottle
perfect for your pub crawls
to the Mermaid, and the mooning
after girls you wouldn't let
yourself have, till later, when
there was always a tit or a bottle
in your mouth if there weren't
words coming out, in booming poems,
or undertones: *Haven't heard*
a bloody word for years, she said.

I understand this. The oral,
and its failure, from the Greek, like
oracle, the fount and font of wisdom,
milk, and beer. And foolishness.
In your wheedling letters to Caitlin,
your begging letters to everyone else,
poems got lost beneath the prose,
while little got said that could be,
no matter how witty that whinging
for money and forgiveness was
because of another bottle, another
breast, until you said so clearly,

I've had eighteen straight whiskeys.
I think that's the record.

And the Welsh set the record
crooked because they wanted
the English to think they knew
something they didn't,
and breasts became mumbles,
hiding the secret in the only safe
they had left, the language.
So that hunger became the hunting
for the right words,
the chewing on words and the past,
and the words of the past,
until the record is straight,
and everything gets said
that should be.

There

The thing about being here
is being everywhere.
So many go to the Great Plains,
the Indians are bumping into us.
But because I'd read so much about them,
I spent the Seventh Century with the Celts,
lived on a hill until the people
wouldn't come near, except to place
big stones around my bed.
Then I'd lie on the stones and watch
the clouds go over, turning light, then dark.
It was so quiet. When I'd go through
the village streets, they'd shudder and look around.
I'd be very still, sit in a corner,
but once I accidentally overturned
a pail of milk and they had a fit.
Later, a priest asked one of them
why they wouldn't go up the hill
to the circle of stones.
Spirits, she said.
You mean angels, the priest said.
Spirits, she said. The priest said,
You're a fool. What a fool, I said,
but only she heard.

The Children of Rhys the Deep

are fairy folk on Rhys, an island
made invisible by an herb,
and only those who bring this plant
growing on a piece of Wales can see
where they live without envy,
obeying all the rules, none unfaithful.
When they speak of a traitor,
they imagine the head of the Devil,
ass's feet, and human hands:
he is usually holding a large knife,
the family dead around him.

The fairies don't come anymore
to buy iron, their only lack,
paying too much, leaving gold and silver
by night on counter and salver.
To them we've become like islands
unseen and alone, only imagined
by all that is invisible.

The Vines

Vines Cottage, Wales, 1996

This year we've lived in stone,
in what our Welsh friend calls
a cowshed, watched the vine
or vines that climb along the walls
and hang above the doors
go gold, with purple grapes,
then bare, then green.
Mornings brought the sheen
of spider webs, dew on the lovespoon
scrollery of trellised roses,
the carpet stitched with silver
traceries of snails,
in frost the filigree of garden hose
about to coil, suspended by its tail.

We thought we knew
exactly where we were, until
we woke, the breadcrumbs gone,
you blaming me, me blaming you,
in a forest dark where ways
we thought we had by heart
diverged or crossed, a maze,
until we nearly came apart.
As good as lost, almost alone,
our single sorrows met and turned
into a footpath doubling back to home,
this cottage, where we've learned
how vines that tangle also twine—
have to, to crush and come to wine.

FOUR

Depth of Field

Forecast

Unsettled conditions continue to cover
the whole of the British Isles,
while a series of troughs, depressions,
will be starting in the west and spreading east
later, though there will be some bright spots,
especially in the south.
Winds northeast backing to north,
light, increasing to fresh to brisk.
After a dry start, early outbreaks of rain,
some heavy, will give way
to mostly sunny weather
with only a few showers,
dying out later when dryer weather
will start in the north and spread.
Showers turning to rain,
though it should be brighter
later, with sunny intervals in the north.
There will be rain in most places.

Hetty Pegler's Tump

The mirror cracked from side to side.
—Alfred Lord Tennyson

After years I remember only the words—
my wife knows the spot on the map.
So we have to make it up: the *tump*,
a sound like beer in a barrel or wine in a tun,
Hetty, found a witch and buried upright,
and Pegler, standing for centuries
on one leg and a stump.

A one-legged woman, then,
in a tump, a tumulus of oak
tangled like hair in the middle of
a hay field (or oats or rye?
Tennyson liked the sound of *barley*
as much as he liked *Shallot*),
a woman waiting to be drawn
out of a barley field, then,
like a sword and made to shine,
instead of staying buried
on the road to Ozzleworth Bottom.

My wife is fuzzy about this,
doesn't remember Hetty existing in time—
coming before the bottom—
only in space, a dark wood
so wet after weeks of rain
we didn't go deeper, just to the first
circle, where the souls stand
with one foot caught in stumps,
condemned of some sin of love,

like her, ugly and deformed,
losing her leg to the hard farm,
maybe mangled by a harrow (her
brothers and father mean to her
from the birth that killed her mother),
losing her soul to the young master
riding by like Lancelot
on his palfrey with sheepdog-hairy,
wine-tun hooves going
tump, tump, tump, tump,
down to the bottom past her hovel,
the sewn, sackcloth curtains parted
slightly, the mirror behind
cracked by the stones of children.

Dorothy's Room

Alfoxton House, Somerset, 1996

I stayed in your room,
your name on the plastic key
in the house where you lived
like a shadow of your famous brother.
Disappointed, I saw his name
on the door down the hall
and caught a glimpse of toilet
through the crack.
The floors creaked.
What might have been your ghost,
waking me, was my wife, naked,
fumbling for pills in moonlight.
I left, I'm afraid,
without seeing you,
you who might have told me
what to do now.
But you wouldn't have me
for husband,
and I wouldn't have you,
with your headaches, corsets,
and sleeplessness.
What a sister, though,
you would have made.
After a life of poems
and long walks, your hand
smoothing my brow, saying
Sweet William, brother,
why did you bother?

Troutbeck

for Jim Houck 1941–1995

fire green as grass
—Dylan Thomas

Where Wordsworth, who is dead,
walked along the beck where trout
rise to stipple the water
for mayflies who only live a day,
and Beatrix Potter colored her sheep
and rabbits, the ancestors of these.

It's so green here, grass
seems to grow on top of grass,
the trees double-dyed.
So green, Jesus, who is dead,
and Plato, too, might have said
this is where green began,
this valley the paint tube squeezed
for green forever, amen.
No wonder Morris and Burne-Jones
stained the glass in the church green—
green Jesus and disciples, green
Marys, all in a Sherwood Forest.
And when the sun shines through, well. . . .

This May the calendar on my wall
opened a window onto that summer,
up the hill a pub, The Mortal Man,
where we ate shepherd's pie
by a turf fire—peat, the past
so packed and pressed a green

fuse of flame spurts out
bright as many summers,
brighter than all the windows of the world
with the sun shining through.

Painswick

The colors this November (spinster, sad
stepsister month, hay hat trimmed
with falling leaves and clad
in holey, woolly, evening coat)
were still so perfect, although so late,
the sun was glad to cut its throat
at dusk and bleed above the hills to say,
How could I have topped today?

If death is the mother of beauty,
she's a widow, rich, rouged, and pearled,
with violet-tinted, silver curls,
leaving behind an orphan world
running naked everywhere,
precocious, sparking, red-haired, new.
She cries each evening in despair,
Child, whatever will become of you?

Under Sir John's Hill

Over Sir John's hill,
The hawk on fire hangs still.
                    —Dylan Thomas

I. Laugharne

Over the stile and molar stones
orange with lichen and yellow with moss,
across the golf-green, sheep-nibbled carpet
littered with placenta and coal-pile droppings,
we're walking Wales again, have flown
all this way to, although we've missed
April and see only limbs
empty of lilac, the red stab wounds
on the dog-belly skin of shorn ewes.
A lamb raises its head to listen,
and goes back to grass.

II. Strathglass

We won't be here much longer,
and may never be back, who knows,
so we're working hard, but it's raining
and has been this whole month,
has been getting ready to rain
for the two years we've been planning,
like the rabbit this morning had been waiting
a whole life to run under the tire
of an American's rental car
in a hollow the trees make between
hedgerows on a road no one uses.
Like high jumpers, we all
had to start on the right foot
years ago for everything
to come out wrong.

III. Lower Slaughter

To see the duck splash and another church,
we stop like Larkin with his bicycle clips,
look through gravestones to find the family name.
The sun comes out for a moment, gilding everything,
throwing rainbows around, and we know
that we'll remember this moment,
though we can't take it in right now,
for the mind won't give you the moment,
but only memory, dry and hard
as money you can only spend
later, if at all.

IV. Stoke

We only have one day of sun,
so I won't go inside, into the dark
factory where they make the beautiful things
from clay and fire them to glaze
like a bone handle.
I stay outside and walk,
where there's not much.
The canal over there goes someplace,
but I circle a pond, the path
under willows, the fields around full
of black and white cows, like a Constable.
The old man tells me there's a pike in here
big as my thigh, but I see only ducks,
hear only something that plops into
the water by the old boathouse, all
roof like a house half drowned.
My holiday over, and this its only day,
I keep trying to remember, keep
circling this dam barely holding
blue sky, perfect clouds, reeds, reflections.

V. Hawkshead

On the path from the church
through darkling wood, a boy
teaches his dog, a mutt, obedience,
makes him stand and wait until
he's out of sight, around the bend.
He may never come back, and the dog
hangs fire, stands taut and trembling,
ears pointed, forever.
Finally,
he's out of the gate
and by us like ten horses,
as if he'd heard something, slight,
like an empty cottage in the hills
with a door open in the wind.

Castle Combe

It's a long way down to the village
from the free car park, through
a tunnel of ancient trees, on a road
worn by the feet and cartwheels of the centuries
till the banks on either side are high
as levees, laced with roots.
Here's where they film Thackeray
and Austen, and everyone's here
for the way it was—the cottages
of golden stone, ivy and roses,
the clear stream with trout and ducks
and waving waterweed, the tonsure
of thatch, no wires or antennae visible.

It's a long way back up,
and we knew each step down
was a debt we'd have to pay.

Remains to Be Seen

Welcome. There's a small fee for photos,
payment for the cob whose arm we laid
cell by stone cell around the spruce-green harbor,
for the cottages of the sailors' widows,
the lifeboat that falls from its notch of cove
into the storm like a log down a flume.
Did you think the thatch grew like moss
the stones piled themselves beneath to raise,
then sprouted from eaves clematis and roses,
that the streets were lava that flowed between houses
and bubbled and hardened into cobbles?
Even the salt air you breathe and return to us
as spray, the mizzle shine of the cat's fur,
the wind that's wizened and cropped our trees
into bonsai, has been bought.
If this recompense seems too dear,
then when the fishermen come back
from their bobbing, if they ever do,
throwing skate still cold from deep
water before your cameras, see
their white bellies, mouths and eyes
still open to the sky,
as the faces of the drowned.

Inverness

Every time we came, the clouds
bruised and lowered, wreathed
the mountains, stewed
the pine-root tannin tea
of lochs and rivers.
Bagpipes clogged and squealed
like piglets stuck and squeezed,
the ground glass of wee midgies rose
from heather and settled in our woollies
and our hair. Twenty years ago,
at this mouth, this *Inver*, of the Ness,
we'd nurse a pub beer for hours by
a good turf fire, while wind
filled the tent with rain,
or flies like a plague of Egypt
found the seams.

Now, the toilet's in the room
with forty channels and remote,
and good malt whisky's everywhere.
Well, what did we expect?
Yea, the whipped cream meets
the scone, and verily the bitter beer
chills and bubbles, red deer run
into the hills or under wheels
of rental cars and coaches driving by
a concrete Nessie, prices rise like mist
amid the candy-colored, toadstool tents of all
the nations sprung from stony ground.

Once we stooped by a lonely road
along the loch and picked

a stone like a dragon's head, then
scanned the purple water, hoping
something might survive,
hiding in the cracks of the world.
Now we know the monster lives—
it rises with a mouth to swallow everything,
all our dreams of wealth come true.

The Silkie

We know what those old songs
and stories really are about—
bairns born wet and cauled
to Shetland maidens visited
by the nameless in the night—
thick black whiskers, slick side
and bullet shape in the green sea
of dream, lingering smell of low tide
in the room, brine in the fur.

And then she marries the harpooner,
a good steady man,
and gets old,
as stories have her held
in swan-foot flippers, down
the seal-king's women taken,
their weed-hair water-waves
on roof the awful house of his,
forever with him dwell in thrall,
memory the surge-light
that pierces gloom of deep sea-hall.

Simmer Dim

On the longest day of the year,
like bee-in-a-bottle memory,
the sound of bagpipes in my ears,
a Scottish bonnet reveille,

pulls me blindly through the slit of tent
to pee in midnight light that slaps my eyes
back open to my life. I squint
and see my fumes of whisky rise

and merge with mist above the fields of sheep.
Not only is this Skye not gone—
the darkness just a dimming, sleep
another waking, sunset now the dawn—

it never left, our quarrel up before
it started, only mad for me to lie
and simmer, summer in her arms, to pour
her honey on the grain and dry

the peat that smokes the taste of stout
and whisky malt, to shake the day
till lads and lasses tumble out,
to wake the squalling music up, to play

a song with fumbling fiddles, drunken drums,
a tune the pie-eyed piper blows
of a night so short it never comes,
a day so long it never goes.

Depth of Field

Careering across Ireland like Toad
on two wheels past signs that say
               Accident
        •
as if Blind Pew has been here
inside this video game that lulls
us up to speed until cresting the hill
we find between stone walls or hedgerows
a hay wain, two kilted schoolgirls, border
collie, stag at bay, pothole and oncoming
petrol truck with Guinnessed driver dying
to let bloom his can of compressed flames.

It can be done.
Everyone shifts a little
and the wind between buffs the finish.
Cloud and rain are moment to moment.
What if we have an accident, we ask
at the airport. *You won't,* they say,
giving us receipts. She has an aneurysm,
my heartbeat's atypical. They call them
punctures, we call them flats.

We used to remember every day of every
trip, didn't need the slides. Now,
we forget where we were yesterday.
Our forgetfulness overtakes us.
They say overtake, we say pass.
Soon, we'll foresee where we'll be,
but forget what we saw.
You'll know when we begin to forget
the future too
by the way our eyes are closed.

FIVE

The Last Holiday

The Last Holiday

Spetses, Greece 1996

Here on the pebbled beach by the wine-dark sea,
we ache for what we know—the white sand and aqua
of the Gulf of Mexico—though light here silvers
the leaftips of the olive trees, grass between
as golden as the autumn vines of Tuscany,
houses bleach like skulls
on the Day of the Dead in Mérida,
and cicadas grind like all the pepper mills
of high season in Provence.
The clothesline flaps its flag of one white shirt:
The Espresso Bean, Cannon Beach, as if to say,
my body went to Oregon, but all I got was memory.
Now, this place too will be the ever youthful
body of another lover we have lost.

How many summers have we left?
Our suntans wrinkle like packed clothes,
our hair grows a sea-salt grizzle,
sunsets bleed in the whites of our eyes.
Perhaps it's not too late to seek another shore,
with pines like these in Cézanne chunks of green,
strung like the sponges of Tarpon Springs,
the water warm as rum, tequila clear,
where we plan to go next year, if we're still alive,
and where, no doubt, we'll pine for Greece
with all of yearning's yin and yang,
as oceans spin their spiral galaxies of shells,
and, down in the garden, lemons
hang like a thousand suns.

White Roads

Like life the ways are wide
and smooth at first, the signs
like arrows aimed into the side

of every new, upcoming town, till lines,
so clear and sanguine on the map, begin
to peter out (*pietro* here) among the vines.

These *stradi importanti,* paved at first, then
turn into *bianco,* talcum roads, and soon our wheels
are dusting grapes and migrant men

who wave us down into the field
and hand us bunches we can barely hold.
We wonder how much wine they'd yield,

how many bottles worth they might have sold.
In the car, they start to must,
as if they were fermenting, old

already, but we eat them just
the way they are, spitting seeds to sprout
along the road and grow in dust.

We think our luck's run out
each morning when we wake to gray,
but then we throw the shutters out

and blink into another autumn day
of sun, just the merest morning chill,
and mist that starts to lift and float away

to wreathe Panzano on a distant hill.
We roll the road, which soon turns white.
Hey, we say, we're lost, but still

we're cavalier, world-weary, quite
the cosmopolitans, but lost, the trees
around us twisted in the Tuscan light

like tusks of boar we never see,
except at dinner, minced, with squid, and ray,
and octopus, and other squirming things we

never eat at home. Already they
are in our cells, as dust is ground
into our skin and lungs to stay,

as in our mouths the sounds,
bon giorno, uno litro, bend
the tongue as smooth and round

as coins we take back home to end
in drawers, like photos of a beauty spot
to bore our friends, make them think we send

the postcards home from where we've been and not
from where our paths are double-crossed
by roads arterial on the map, but when we've got

to drive them, ghostly, white as frost,
as chalk that rises like a second birth
of rock that, drifting after us, is lost

and will not lift and leave the earth
but lingers, clings to what has died,
to flesh for all its worth.

In the Musée d'Orsay

About suffering, they were never wrong,
the Old Masters. . . .

—W. H. Auden

We flail our bodies along, legs
        failing, arches falling, but we've never
seen such light, tint, and tone at once,
        the sky gushing through the ribs of steel
to show each Cézanne and Van Gogh,
        in a line along the wall, no darker than the real
windows to the France outside, Montmartre,
        mount of martyrs on the hill
across the Seine, bleached in sun like a cemetery,
        the sky deep blue above the Sacre Coeur
with orange Magritte hot-air balloons
        and puffy bruised-on-the-bottom clouds.

Raised a temple to the train, then
        almost razed, the bones were resurrected,
the skeleton was saved and given
        new transparent flesh.
Through the crystal ceiling and
        high windows everywhere,
light falls past us to the ground
        where sculptures writhe, held down
by stone that lends its form
        to all their yearning.

We should stop before we kill ourselves,
        and we have to pee *again,*
and it's always in the basement,
        but there's also always one more room

of air and color, and a greedy childish
    clarity still intact inside
drags us to another sunlit day in Arles,
    its wrung-out cypresses squirming up,
or the stony mount of gauzy St. Victoire,
    till we are down, but still not out,
crawling towards another bright Monet
    mirage of river, sea, and sky,
    gasping, *water, water* as we die.

In the Old Neighborhood

When I walk through the door, light
hits off bleached oyster shells,
and the fan in the moldy clapboard wall
blows the kitchen air of fried shrimp out.
I'm less remembering
than wading through the past,
the way I once moved through
those hot and cold spots in the Gulf
when I used to fish the surf.
Here, at this corner, something happened,
its honeysuckle, its sticky air,
live oak shade pulling at the outlines.
In one of these dark pools
over deep springs, my temperature drops
into an old love. I step into the
prickling sun of her skin, smell
the mountain of sugar cane husks
rotting across the river—
ghosts of warm greens and yellows,
cool purples of cloud and tree shadow
that blow down the river to the Gulf
and begin to move in the tides.

Hooks

In the Gulf, where my wife almost died
one day, crabbing in the hot sun,
and where that Kate Chopin heroine waded out
to drown herself, I caught a banana fish,
the Daffy Duck of the sea. When I made
the rookie mistake of keeping the rod bent,
the fish dithered and threw the hook into my thumb.
I remembered movies about Indians and arrows,
and tried to push it through, to cut off
the barb, but the edges of my sight grew black,
like a crepe-hung portrait of a thumb.

Along the bayou, across the salt marsh,
my wife drove as I lay in the back seat, where
she would lie two years later, vessels
about to burst in her brain.
As we drove over bridges of fishermen
who didn't even know they were happy,
I thought of mountain men dragging bear-broken legs
miles to trading posts, and felt weak and silly,
and then, when we got to the hospital in Golden Meadow,
humiliated when the Cajun nurse said, *You muss not be
from around heah*, and I looked at the big board under glass,
all of the hooks and lures pulled out,
and from what parts of the tourist body,
and they were all there—earlobes,
balls, eyelids, eyeballs. Once, long
after all this, I clipped from the newspaper
the story of a man standing behind his wife
when she cast. *It hurt so bad*, he said,
I couldn't even yell, so his wife pulled back

and gave another yank. It took hours
of surgery to dig out that treble hook.

My wife didn't die, I'm happy
to report, and I became a better person,
I think. So that's why, after the doctor
gave me my shot and pulled with a sound
like a leaf tearing, what he held up
I see now as a kind of symbol, like a bullet
wearing a hula skirt.

Creature

We kayak through the mangroves
over only inches of water,
over stingrays and horseshoe crabs,
the spined and slimy things
of a million years.
Old fishes too, pelagic, bony,
the bottom-feeders: choupique, snook,
alligator gar, and gaspergou,
snapping turtle the Cajuns
find with their feet,
the spikes of the leather back
pointed away from the bladed beak.

I've never trusted what's beneath
the surface, what your foot can find,
since in the dark of the Grove Theater
I saw what Julie Adams couldn't,
what was watching her swimming,
reaching up its webbed paw
toward the shapely kicking leg
to touch with a claw her heel.
Who goes swimming in a black lagoon?
And sure enough, they got stuck there,
waiting for it to come for them.

But really it was Silver Springs,
clear to the bottom where smiling
mermaids suck on air hoses,
and the studio Universal.
Maybe that's why I'm on a real lagoon,
suspended on tea-dark water over
God knows what, a long blind walk

over razor clam and oyster shell,
through slime and spine to shore.
I think I pray for flotation,
that my feet touch nothing more
than water, though what I see
is mangroves, how
like spiders they put down
all of their legs,
feeling for bottom.

Dancing with Sharks

On the Gulf coast of Florida,
       the sharks come in at night, maybe
drawn by the candlelights of seafood
       dinners, through the reefs, trolling
the shoals, the troughs between the waves,
       cruising sandbars for the flesh from shells,
the odd, lonely fish-softness of whatever they smell.

       After dinner of fresh snapper with limes,
we shuck our clothes, go down
       to bob in the warm waves,
our feet barely touching bottom.
       We've seen them caught, know
they're here, five- and six-footers,
       but we hold each other and dance,
pressing close in the salty dark
       gumbo-thick with plankton and the spray
of a trillion eggs like the stars overhead.
       And when I enter the oyster folds
of her, we feel things sliding
       between our legs, restless
with their slick skins
       and endless appetites.

Blind River

I walk the sandy road, that strip
of grass in the middle like a church aisle.
Spanish moss beards the path,
gloom of swamp on my left.
In the bayou on my right, crawfish,
catfish, and cottonmouths barely move,
doze in the hot water green with scum
and water lilies, though the bottoms
of my feet are cool on the shady, oyster shell road,
mosquitoes a dial tone in my ears,
1-800-The Past.

I don't live here anymore—it's just
the road I travel home each night, the dark
water I wade into before sleep,
beyond the shades and blinds,
sulfurous lights on snow and city streets.

Progress

. . . but the way is the way, and there is an end.
—John Bunyan

Trying to forget the growing spot my mother
called my strawberry, the place, she said,
a fairy finger blessed, and afraid there may not be another
Thanksgiving, I get it in my head

to hunt some woods, the kind
I played in forty years ago, alone
from sun till star, and finally find,
by climbing through barbed wire and stone,

the closest thing to woods these days,
a bulldozed trail that's marking out
roads and circles and drives and ways
destined to be Otter, Eagle, Oak, or Trout.

I follow the spindly, snapstick path, the rut
through lodgepoles of only a decade's girth
since the last big trees were clear-cut,
felled, milled, and gone from the gullied earth.

These spots are growing, too, the seeds
blowing on every wind—an emptiness scatters.
Here is no knowing what anything needs
or caring how much what's gone matters.

I actually see a deer, her white flag high,
and a turkey running toward the swamp to hide,
but they're already stranded on this island by
the highways swelling on every side.

This future road keeps forking, *if the fates allow.*
Though not yet lost or traveling through the dark,
I pass where beavers try to dam the slough
but the locals tear it up; the park

must have its skiing lake, and so they trap or kill
them. Beavers, like the pines, don't know
the jig is up. They'll keep on gnawing till
they're stopped, going where they have to go,

as I've always followed where the roads have led,
the more- or less-traveled, feeling my way,
sometimes on needles soft as any bed,
sometimes down to the pumpkin-colored clay.

Cavan Girl

St. Patrick's Day was a good one
to bury an Irish girl from Georgia,
her grandfather a Sheridan, nice, she said,
most of the time, except when he'd go
on a "bat." I imagined
hitting something hard
and running the bases for days.
Once they found him trying to swim
across the lake at Lakewood Park.

At Mother's funeral, my aunt
could just barely remember
their grandmother's name, Emma Wiggins,
and how she waited, rocking on the porch,
sure that someone would find him
and bring him home, just like he found *her*
on the crowded boat to Ellis Island,
though they came from the same county.

I flew from Wales for the funeral
to see her laid beside my father,
behind what used to be woods,
but now a Waffle House,
the crematorium with columns like Tara,
fruit trees everywhere flowering white.

Before we took my mother's keys away,
she'd show up for Sunday morning
on Tuesday night, and, in her best clothes,
walk across the empty parking lot
and into the dark church.

Or on a "tear," she'd say bitterly,
as if he needed some complete
rupture, if not a lake, then a mountain,
or a woman.

I never went to see her in the home,
not that she would have known me.
My wife said the other night,
It's just that I haven't seen you
drinking this late in a long time.

The police brought him home, wet,
and laid him on the porch. *Tom Sheridan?*
they asked, and while Mother stood
behind the screen, Emma nodded
to show them who he was
and where he belonged.

Return Journey

With twenty miles left, I think
home free, but then remember
that morning coming back from Florida,
how we drove all night so we could stay
and swim just one more day,
all the neon stations closed, the needle
sinking, the Fairlane sputtering down
to die in a suburban street at five A.M.
with half a mile to go.

My family now is dead
or gone, maybe that the last
holiday we had together,
and why we weren't more cranky,
as if we knew. I hope so—
running out of gas and walking
slowly back to the weedy yard
of all our woes.

If anyone was up that early,
drinking coffee, looking idly out,
they must have seen a dreamy, backwards sight:
beyond their freshly shaven lawn,
a family, clutching pillows tight,
laughing, walking toward the dawn.

ABOUT THE AUTHOR

William Greenway, a native of Georgia with a BA from Georgia State University and a PhD from Tulane University, is a professor of English at Youngstown State University. He has published two chapbooks and three full-length collections of poetry, most recently *How the Dead Bury the Dead* in the Akron Series in Poetry.

ABOUT THE BOOK

Simmer Dim was designed and typeset by Kachergis Book Design of Pittsboro, North Carolina. The typeface, Columbus MT, was designed by Patricia Saunders for Monotype Typography in 1992. *Simmer Dim* was printed on 60-pound Glatfelter Natural and bound by Cushing-Malloy of Ann Arbor, Michigan.